The United

By Cameron Jamieson

Jamieson, Cameron

The United States of Australia: an Aussie bloke explains Australian to Americans

ISBN-13: 978-1508443766
ISBN-10: 1508443769

To my wife Sarah;
Living proof that America is beautiful

Spelling Warning

This book uses Australian-English spelling in order to prepare you for your trip Down Under.

While it may be upsetting to realise that American-English is not universal you will never-the-less be able to get your head around the menu and inflight magazine on your Qantas Airways flight to Sydney.

(Get the hint? Buy a Qantas ticket NOW)

About the Author

Cameron Jamieson is a quintessential Aussie Bloke. That is, he speaks his mind, is passionately Australian, is down-to-earth and, above all, he does not drink Foster's Lager beer.

Born in 1965, Cameron left school at the age of 15 to become a labourer because it was the social expectation at the time. Thanks to an Australian Army career of over 30 years (full and part-time) he has met thousands of Americans, including his beautiful wife when they served together on a US Navy-led humanitarian mission in Southeast Asia in 2012.

In the 1990s Cameron completed a journalism degree with the University of Western Sydney. This allowed him to start his life-long dream of pursuing writing as a vocation.

You can chat with the author and keep up to date with his latest work and images at:

www.facebook.com/CameronAshleyJamiesonAuthor

Maps

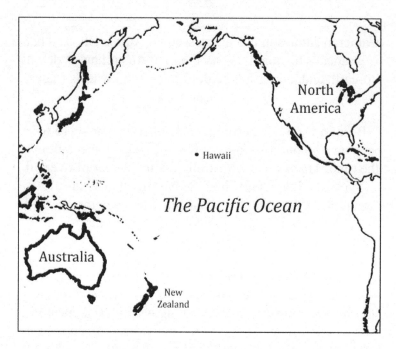

Map1: A Bloke's guide to the Pacific Ocean

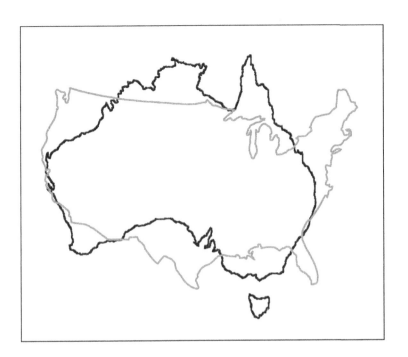

Map 2: Australia and the US Lower 48 States landmasses compared

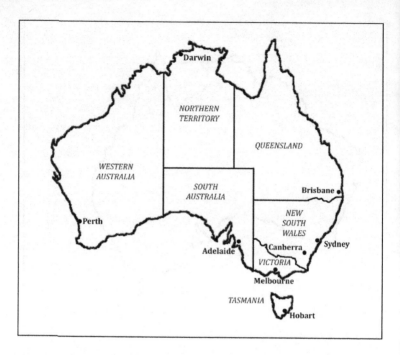

Map 3: Australian states and major cities

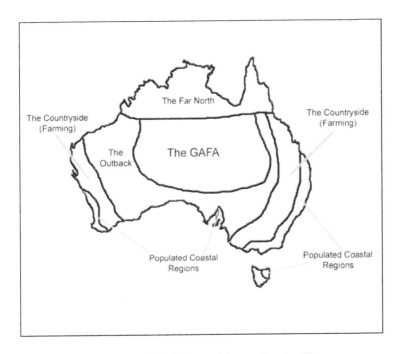

Map 4: A Bloke's guide to Australia

Table of Contents

Preface

G'day. My life in Australia has been spent immersed in American culture. Like maple syrup over a stack of pancakes I have seen how U.S. movies, TV, music, cars, and computer systems have seeped into the crevices of everyday Aussie life to create a flavoursome coating to our British core.

To be fair, Australia is a multicultural country where all are welcome. We have a noble and ancient indigenous culture at our very heart, and the extent to which we have embraced other nationalities is exemplified by our never-ending variety of foreign food restaurants in every city.

However it is the American influence that now underwrites our freedom and interpretation of the world.

I have been fortunate throughout my 30-year Australian Army career to work alongside thousands of US military personnel. My home is full of US culture and gadgets, and I have been extremely lucky to marry a beautiful American woman who serves as a constant reminder of how America makes the world a much better place.

I am struck at the number of Americans I have spoken with who would like to travel to Australia yet know so little about the Great Southern Land. It is with this in mind that I write this book. Not that my irreverent stories are particularly useful as a tourism guide, however I hope that my insights into what makes Australia and Australians tick will allow you to embrace us Aussies with the inside knowledge needed to avoid being treated like a clueless foreigner once you get here.

The following chapters also describe my interpretation of how Australians view America and Americans, and there are also some tips for understanding those of us from The

Land Down Under who talk through their nose at a frightening pace.

Some of it is meant to be funny, some of it is just my observations and some is serious because some topics are not funny to talk about. I hope you find these dialogs entertaining none-the-less, and if you do make it to our sun-drenched shores then I am looking forward to an opportunity to meet you and share a laugh and a beer.

As a word of warning though, these are my meanderings and should not be considered as factual – if you want facts please consult Wikipedia.

Cameron Jamieson

Chapter 1: The Changeover

Being an Australian nowadays is to live a life of colliding cultures.

We are a great mixture of Aboriginal and migrant cultures, but the ones that pervade the most are British and the US of A.

In the beginning the Land of Oz was populated by a noble indigenous population. This changed in the late 18th Century when the British decided to take a look at the place after some surly Yanks invited the Brits to pack up their gear and get the hell out of their American colony.

You see, the British needed a place to dump convicts and raise a bit of revenue. There wasn't much of an international legal framework back then so the British conveniently labelled Australia as vacant land and moved in.

To make sure of things though, first the British sent a rather small ship and its crew to take a look at the joint. This reconnaissance to the southern seas was undertaken by a bloke by the name of James Cook, the same fellow who later sailed around Alaska for a bit and then died when he found out that Hawaiians are fickle when it comes to visitors.

Back in England after his first voyage of discovery, Cook and his esteemed team's glowing report led to the go-ahead for a first fleet shipment of convicts to the new southern land, and despite some rough years the various colonies grew prosperous and were later united to form Australia on January 1st, 1901.

However, although the umbilical cord had been cut, we were still tied to mother's apron strings. We were very,

very British and we paid a terrible toll with our troops when they supported the mother country in World War 1.

And we continued to consider ourselves British, right up until Pearl Harbour. Then things changed.

At the same time the Japs were attacking the US ships in Hawaii the Royal Australian Air Force was using American-made Lockheed Hudson bombers to attack invading Japanese shipping off Malaya (now Malaysia).

With the invasion of Oz looking uncomfortably likely, and with little prospect of help from Britain, Australia looked to the US for salvation, and you guys delivered.

The US and Australia fought as allies in the air and on the land and sea, driving the fanatical Japs back to where they came from. And we've pretty much been fighting alongside you ever since.

The presence of large amounts of US troops and war machinery in Australia during World War 2 forever changed Aussie culture, and the advent of rock and roll, television and American domination of the Australian car manufacturing business meant the US invasion was complete.

And I'm not complaining. My life is the better for it.

Take for example the night I met for the first time the woman who would become my wife. In 2012 I was a member of the Australian Defence Force contingent to Pacific Partnership, the US Navy-led annual multinational humanitarian aid commitment to the Southwest Pacific and Southeast Asia. It was in the wee-hours of a muggy May night on tropical Guam when our contingent arrived at the US Navy base to board out floating home, the gargantuan US Navy Ship Mercy, a converted super-tanker now a white-painted 1000-bed hospital ship with all the bells and whistles fitted.

Stepping into that ship was like stepping into my TV set – all I could hear was American voices. I've never felt more at home in my life.

We were assigned to our accommodation according to rank, and as I stumbled around the never-ending passageways trying to find 'Officer Country' I walked passed a short, beautiful red-hair civilian volunteer nurse. She caught my eye, and not too long after that she caught my heart with her savoir-faire and American accent. Take it from me; you Yanks really know how to ambush a guy. All I had to do was spend a little time with her and I was hooked for life.

Mind you, while Australia and the US are thriving democracies, there is one thing noticeably different about you Americans and us Aussies and that is that you lot always seem to be in an infernal rush. This became very clear to me one time in 2008 while travelling on the patrol boat USS *Whirlwind* in the North Arabian Gulf.

My Australian Army photographer and I needed a lift to visit an Aussie Navy Commodore who was commanding the Coalition Naval Force protecting the Iraqi off-shore oil platforms from terrorist attack. The US Navy crew of the *Whirlwind* were great Blokes and went to great lengths to make us Aussies feel at home aboard their vessel.

We tootled along through the dusty Arabic air that clung to the gulf's waters and being in the need for some clean air I went below to the Sailor's Mess to make myself a coffee. I was surprised to see off-duty men watching a Mel Gibson movie called The Patriot.

Now Mel is a funny guy – he was born in the US but when he does well we in Australia like to think of him as one of our own – after all, he grew up here and got his acting break and initial stardom here. But when he stuffs up we call him an American. It's convenient.

Anyhow, this movie is about the American Revolutionary War. So I casually remarked to a nearby sailor the following words:

"You know, you Americans fought a bloody and costly war to gain your independence from Britain, but we Australians took our time and eventually became a federated Commonwealth nation by an act of the British Parliament. Not a shot was fired."

The sailor calmly turned and looked at me as if I was the biggest idiot in the world and said, "Well, we Americans are in more of a hurry than you guys…"

Anyhow, I guess you could say I live in a very different Australia to the frightfully British land my grandparents grew up in. We still maintain good ties with the old mother country and we still enjoy a lot of their culture, but we are no longer solely tied up to the British and the Commonwealth of Nations.

The Australia I have known all through my middle-aged life is the product of the US-alliance changeover and as such my life is totally interwoven with stars and stripes. It's in my house, my TV, my iPod, my marriage and my destiny.

And that's OK. While we are definitely not the 51st US state, we regard you Yanks as best mates.

That's high praise from us.

Chapter 2: Blokes and Sheilas

It will probably come as no surprise to you Americans that we Aussies do have a rather different way of talking about things, especially about ourselves.

Welcome to the land of Blokes and Sheilas. I guess I better explain these terms to you.

I'll start with 'Bloke' because it is less controversial; it is still widely used and easier to explain.

'Bloke' is an informal word for an ordinary Australian man. An old British word, it symbolises the common earthiness, toughness and goodness that have become the Australian man's identity through the last couple of centuries.

Given the modern trend for the global homogenising of an individual's identity this image of a Bloke is perhaps more perceived than actual, however the qualities of a Bloke still rise to the surface when an Aussie man is faced with a crisis or he is relaxing among mates.

A famous description of what makes a Bloke was given by the great Australian historian Russel Ward in his 1958 book 'The Australian Legend'. I will share it with you because Ward was a far cleverer bugger than I'll ever be. He described an Australian man as:

"A practical man, rough and ready in his manners and quick to decry any appearance of affectation in others. He is a great improviser, ever willing 'to have a go' at anything, but ... content with a task done in a way that is 'near enough'. Though capable of great exertion in an emergency, he normally feels no impulse to work hard without good cause. He swears hard and consistently, gambles heavily and often, and drinks deeply on occasion.

"He is a 'hard case', sceptical about the value of religion and of intellectual and cultural pursuits generally. He believes that [he] is not only as good as his master but ... probably a good deal better ... He is a fiercely independent person who hates officiousness and authority ... Yet he is very hospitable and ... will stick to his mates through thick and thin, even if he thinks they may be in the wrong."

Nowadays though, reckless gambling and drinking is frowned upon because of its impact on the family. Which isn't a bad thing, all things considered?

A bloke still has to be tough and not put up with crap from idiots. He still uses colourful language but will refrain from swearing in front of women and children when he can help it. He can be relied upon in a crisis but when confronted with the choice of mowing the lawn or going to the beach then the call of the salt water will win every time. He will do the job assigned to him but he may stop when things are 'close enough for government work'.

There is no controversy about being a bloke, but some wankers (i.e. someone who prefers to enjoy sex on their own because they love themselves so much) think they are too good to be labelled a common Bloke. It doesn't matter because this is why the rest of us call them wankers. Honestly, it is the highest honour possible for an Australian man to be considered a good bloke. Enough said.

I'll talk next about the word 'Sheila' but it comes with a warning – not every woman likes it. Some do and they are usually lovely girls with a great sense of humour. Some women think it is derogatory even though it is meant to be a compliment. Let me explain.

Basically, the term 'Sheila' is an Australian slang word for a woman. It was very common last century and it is said to come from the Latin word 'Caelia', which means 'heavenly' or 'of the heavens'. Sheila isn't used as much nowadays, especially compared to 'Bloke', but you do hear it. Personally, if I was a woman and men called me 'heavenly' all day long I'd be happier than a cat with a can-opener at the fish factory.

More specifically, Sheila refers to a woman, often young and single, who is a really good sport. She is happy, of modest means and doesn't mind hanging out with the blokes to watch a bit of cricket or footy (i.e. Australian variations of football played with an oval-shaped ball). She is easy on the eye, which means pretty, but that is a very open term. You don't have to be stick-thin and covered with make-up to be an attractive lass in Australia. In fact, we do like our women to be a healthy weight and have no makeup on at all. Beauty is still in the eye of the beholder.

So, the ultimate goal of any Australian woman should be to be an 'alright sort of Sheila'. Alas, this is not the case because some women have historically linked Sheila with being 'common' and hence illiterate or ungraceful. There are also women who consider Sheila to be another word for 'prostitute'. That is unfortunate, wrong and misses the true meaning of the world but I guess you Yanks are familiar with the concept that perception always beats reality.

The origins for the use of Sheila in Australia is said to come from the Irish who were particularly noticeable as immigrants in the 18th Century. When I studied Australian history at university I distinctly remember reading a British report from the period that said too many Irish people were immigrating to Australia, ruining the Government's plan to stock the Australian colonies with more 'desirable' English well-to-do bloodstock.

Well, two hundred years later we are the better for the migration of the common folk, so the English can go cry in their warm beer and dream of what it must be like to live in a land filled with sunlight and drinking cold beer on a hot day by the pool.

Anyway, 'Sheila' was a fairly popular Irish name and became synonymous for an Irishwoman in the same way as 'Paddy' is synonymous for an Irishman. Eventually the word Sheila began to be used to refer to a good woman regardless of ethnicity and it remains so today.

Now, if you really want to insult an Australian woman then call her a Mole, but prepare to run real fast because you are about to die. Mole is ten times worse than Bitch because Mole is Australian derogatory slang for a woman of loose sexual morals. It was been around in the UK since the early 1600s when then name "Moll" (derived from "Molly") was used as a substitute for 'whore' or 'prostitute'.

Now that I have taught you the ultimate Australian insult for a woman I guess it's time to wrap this chapter up with some summary points:

a. The highest honour possible for an Australian man is to be considered a good Bloke; and

b. Australia is full of great Sheilas but be careful who you say it to. Test the waters, and if you get a smile then you know that the woman you are talking to is the salt of the earth. If you get a frown then remember to not poke the bear anymore if you want to live.

Here endeth the lesson.

Chapter 3: The GAFA

There's a funny thing about you Americans.

It seems that because you live in a big country that's full of stuff then there is no real need to travel overseas. I understand that according to US State Department statistics only about 46% of Americans currently have valid passports.

That means half of your population couldn't give a toss about the rest of the world, and that's fair enough.

After all, there are more than a few people out there who would like to take a pot-shot at an American or take you hostage just because you are from the land of the free. They also speak a lot of funny languages out there in the world, and even I have to agree that I don't want to visit a country that doesn't sell Reese's peanut butter cups.

So the idea that America has pretty much everything you need is fairly logical (and, quite frankly, safe). But I tell you what, you are missing out on a bonza (fantastic) time if you don't visit the land of kangaroos and gum trees at least once in your life. As an added bonus we also speak a version of English, we don't shoot Americans and we sell Reese's peanut butter cups.

How can you argue with that?

I guess one key problem is that most Yanks don't know much about Australia. After all, we have a small population of around 23 million Blokes and Sheilas compared to your whopping-great 316 million peeps. To put that in perspective, the entire Australian population is less than the Texas population of 26 million people. Just think; you could replace every Texan with an Aussie and still have room for three million more Mexicans.

Anyway, being such a small population you could be excused for thinking Australia is a small ex-British outpost somewhere to the southwest of Hawaii (and no, we are not in Europe – that's Austria).

Have a look at Map 1 in the front of this book – we are in the bottom-left corner of the Pacific Ocean (please don't confuse us with New Zealand, they are the small ex-British outpost somewhere to the southwest of Hawaii).

Next, take a look of Map 2, which features an outline of Australia (including Tassie [Tasmania], the funny triangular island to the south) superimposed over the Lower 48 States. You may notice we are about as big as your bit of real estate wedged between Canada and Mexico (Australia is 2.97 million square miles in size versus the Lower 48's 3.12 million square miles).

"But hang on a minute!" I hear you say. How come Australia's population is less than 10% of the US population?

That's a good question, and I'm here to give you the good oil (i.e. I'll give you some rather valuable information).

It has a lot to do with The GAFA.

I'll get to The GAFA in a minute. Take a look at Map 4. I've drawn it myself, so it may not be accurate but its close enough for government work.

You will first notice that the majority of the Australian population lives in the southern half of the country on The Coast, and that's a cool idea as we do have some of the best beaches in the world. It also has a lot to do with the original colonisation of Australia – they set up the towns where the sailing boats could get to. Seeing as you Yanks hadn't yet invented the motorway we decided to keep living near the sea and drink beer. It was a bloody good idea, quite frankly, and it still works for us.

The lower east coast and a bit of Tassie were settled first, followed by a bit on the southwest coast of Western Australia and a bit on the south coast of South Australia. That's how it started and that's how we stayed.

Another reason we stayed close to the coast was because of The Bush, which spreads from the coast to the countryside. Quite frankly, The Bush is a pain in the arse (arse is the same as ass, we just spell it better) to navigate through, so it's best left to the koalas and poisonous snakes to rapturously frolic in. Even the Kangaroos prefer the grasslands. They may hop for a living but they aren't stupid.

Moving inland is The Countryside, where the Cow-Cockeys (farmers) live. This place is OK except there are not many beaches, and farming takes up a lot of land without the need for a lot of people. Plus country music tends to drive most people back to The Coast, so that explains why there aren't many people in The Countryside.

Next, take a gander (i.e. please have a look at) at The Far North of Australia. This place is also a pain in the arse. For example, you can't go into the ocean because:

a.   The Gotcha Fish (i.e. sharks) will get you;

b.   If the Gotcha Fish don't get you then the Gotcha Lizards (i.e. Saltwater Crocodiles) will get you; and

c.   If the Gotcha Lizards don't get you then the Gotcha Jellyfish (i.e. venomous Box Jellyfish) will get you.

So if you walk off the beach and into the sea in the north you are basically dead. The weather isn't much better. This is because being sub-tropical there are only two seasons:

a.   The Dry Season, where you sit and spend six months inside your house with the air conditioning on and wait for it to rain because it is too hot to go outside; and

b.   The Wet Season, where you sit and spend six months inside your house with the air conditioning on and wait for it stop raining because it is too wet and humid to go outside.

It's not a whole lot of fun if you catch my drift.

Also, the Far North countryside is hot, rugged and a bugger of a place to live. So being the sensible people we are, most Aussies don't live there either, but some do.

Most of the hardy souls who reside up north live in and around the coastal city of Darwin (see Map 3). This is the same place that was bombed by the same Japanese fleet that hit Pearl Harbour. I once read a book by an Australian navigator on a tramp-streamer that use to visit Darwin before the Second World War. He reckoned that the main export commodity of the town back then was empty beer kegs.

Quite frankly, not a lot has changed.

If you think of it, the only way to stay sane in Darwin is to sit in front of a fan and drink gallons of mid-strength beer (not full-strength beer - that would be silly). So they do it with great gusto.

To be fair though, The Far North is a fisherman's paradise. Just make sure you have a boat with sides high enough to keep out the Gotcha Fish, Gotcha Lizards and Gotcha Jellyfish. Otherwise your day might get ruined.

Now, let's get to the heart of the matter and to the heart of Australia too. This is where you will find The GAFA.

Now to put it bluntly, the name GAFA is an acronym –
it means the Great Australian F*ck-All. It's called that
because there is F*ck-All out there (i.e. nothing).

Take it from me as I have driven across it a few times.
Once you have driven for 10 miles you have seen it all for
the next 1,000 miles. Honestly, it's enough to drive you
mad and make you steer your car into a billabong (i.e. a
small swamp) to drown.

So now you get the picture. Between The GAFA, The
Far North, The Countryside and The Bush there are not a
lot of nice places to set up your mansion. It's all wonderful
and adventurous to visit, but you wouldn't want to live
there.

This means that there is not a lot of human development
across much of Australia, which keeps our population
small, unlike you Americans who would build a city next to
a salt lake and call it Salt Lake City if given the
opportunity.

However, this doesn't mean you shouldn't visit
Australia. *Au Contraire!*

The two things that make Australia worth visiting
(besides a quick trip to the interior to make you feel like the
world's greatest adventurer) are the people and the wildlife.

If truth be told, Australians are the most laid-back
people in the world. As the saying goes, if we were any
more laid back we'd be sleeping (you may notice that our
Koalas have taken this extra step). We are bloody friendly
people and we produce heaps of world-class beer and wine,
so we have plenty to share with visiting mates.

Also, our native animals are downright hilarious
(forgetting the poisonous snakes and spiders).

Just look at the wombat, platypus, koala and kangaroo. They just go to prove that God has a sense of humour.

So if I were you I'd grab a passport, jump on the Flying Kangaroo (i.e. Qantas Airways) from Los Angeles and get your arse over to Australian quick-smart. You'll have the time of your life with friendly people and silly wildlife, we won't make you stay in The GAFA and we'll have the booze ready and waiting for you.

Just don't ask about the spiders and snakes.

Chapter 4: Mates and Cobbers

If you know anything about Australia it's probably that we call everyone 'mate'.

We even say it to the ladies, although I am a bit uncomfortable about that because I don't want every woman to think I want to mate with them. I do, however, want to be polite and friendly because that's how we are as Australians.

To get your head around this idea of mateship you just need to understand the following concept: America is 'the land of opportunity' while Australia is 'the land of equality'.

You see, we genuinely look upon each other as equals. I have had the honour to meet several of our Prime Ministers and when you look them in the eye and say 'G'day' as you shake their hand you just know you could be talking across the fence to your neighbour.

The word 'mate' in Australia means 'friend' regardless of if you have known someone for 10 years or 10 seconds. Its prolific use found its origins in the shared hardships encountered by migrants following European settlement in Australia from 1788 onwards. Mateship also firmly extends to our indigenous population, who from my experience are some of the most gentle and funniest people in the world.

The early bonds of Aussie mateship were also a direct backlash against the rigid class structure of Britain and Europe from which most of our convicts and free settlers were trying to escape (just like the immigrants moving to the US at the same time). Mateship was further reinforced on the goldfields where a gold digger's life was hard and interdependent with those that shared this tough itinerant life.

There was still the presence of upper-class in the ruling political and military elite within the Australian colonies as these officials had come to do these duties directly from Britain before returning home to their pompous social bubble. For those of us who stayed 'egalitarianism' became the name of the game and it remains that way today.

National mateship was firmly cemented by the Australian experience of war, particularly in World War 1, to the point where it has become a stated military virtue. The inherent mateship that abounded in our fledgling army strengthened the soldier's sense of family, welfare and the notion they could count on each other under the worst possible conditions.

One example that always brings a lump to my throat was recorded by Australia's official military historian Charles Bean prior to an assault on Turkey's Gallipoli peninsular in 1915 at the Battle of Lone Pine, one of the most famous battles in Australia's military history.

In the darkness the troops waited for the order to launch themselves from their frontline trench and race across open ground to capture the fortified Turkish trenches. Many did not survive the crossing and ensuing hand-to-hand combat.

Against this backdrop of awkward pre-battle silence a soldier arrived at his designated section of the Australian trench and, according to Bean, the following dialogue occurred:

'Jim here?' he asked.
A voice in the fire step answered, 'Right here Bill'.
'Do you chaps mind movin' up a piece?' asked the first voice.
'Him and me are mates - and we're goin' over together'.

Our military mateship was also extended to our Allies and others, including to the US troops who we first fought and died alongside of at the successful Battle of Hamel in Northern France in 1918. Our broadening offer of soldier's mateship also helped to break down racial stereotypes. For example, in the horrific Papua New Guinea campaign of World War 2 we relied heavily on native porters to carry ammunition and supplies forward and carry our wounded back to the rear over the near-vertical treacherous and narrow muddy mountain trails that hallmarked the campaign.

We called these men the 'Fuzzie-Wuzzie Angels' because of their native hairstyles, a nickname given with great affection and still revered to this day across Australia. Even military working dogs have become our best mates since the Vietnam War due to their dedication to duty and their lifesaving work. To this very day the work of these dogs is nationally applauded and the loss of a dog in action in places like Iraq and Afghanistan is still a cause for public mourning.

What's truly terrific about the evolution of Australia's mateship culture is that the despicable racist attitudes of the nation's white population in years gone past have been eroded by modern common sense. After all, no-one has any say over who their parents are, so you have no say in your ethnicity, your skin colour or even what colour eyes you have. Therefore what do these things matter if it is beyond your control?

What really matters is that you do have a say in how you act within Australian society. If you are a thief, troublemaker, loudmouth, radical bull-shit-artist or even a plain-old dickhead then you deserve the bad tidings and misery that are coming your way. If you are a good and fair person then you will be treated like you are the salt of the earth regardless of your racial background, sexual orientation, religion or political views.

Another old Australian word used by men to describe a friend or a companion is 'Cobber'. Cobber has been traced back to 1890s and is the thought to come from the British expression 'cob' which means to take a liking to someone.

Cobber is rarely used by young people nowadays but I am one of the old and bold die-hard Aussie's trying to keep it in common use. This is because, once again, it has strong military links, particularly with World Wars 1 and 2.

During these wars the term 'Cobber' came to mean something more than a mate. It signified that someone was your best mate, someone you were willing to take a bullet for. I feel strongly about this so I try to promote this version of the word.

Now, I do sometimes call people 'Cobber' just for a bit of a smile, but I only say it seriously to a select few people. I don't call my wife and children Cobbers because it's unnecessary – it's only natural that I would sacrifice myself for them.

Likewise I don't call other women and children Cobbers even though I would not hesitate to protect them with my life, whether I knew them or not, because it's the gentlemanly thing to do.

I would only use the word Cobber properly to describe those special friends, be they still in the military, retired veterans I served with or civilian friends who are very dear to me.

They know who they are, so enough is said. All I can add is that I have many American mates and a few American Cobbers. I hope you can make a few Australian Cobbers too.

Chapter 5: Bloody Fosters

It's because I like you Americans so much that I am going to let you in on one of Australia's most closely guarded secrets.

Aussies don't drink Foster's Lager beer.

Now this may come as a big surprise to you but the fact is plain and simple: it tastes bland. We Aussies like a bit more flavour in our national drink.

So why do we make it? It's because we earn a fortune selling it to visiting tourists and in foreign countries where the concept of a good tasting beer doesn't exist.

It wasn't always like that though. I distinctly remember as a young man in the early 1980s drinking Foster's at the local pub with my best mate Slim. Back then Foster's wasn't world famous and it wasn't brewed in recycled super-tankers. So the flavour was more traditional, refreshing and slid down the throat very nicely.

In fact Slim and I invented a new drink called a Bloody Foster's. We'd start a night by grabbing a big glass of ice-cold Foster's from the bar along with a small glass of tomato juice. We'd drink a bit of beer to make room for the tomato juice, add the juice and hey presto – a Bloody Foster's!

We figured this was a healthy way to start the night, combining the much-needed vitamins to our favourite beer. Such is the genius of youth.

Unfortunately for us Foster's really took off around the world and the resulting massive brewing expansion meant the beer had to be standardised for manufacture in other countries under licence. It lost its homely flavour, it became homogenised and bland and so we said farewell to an old friend.

Mind you, the brewery didn't care. The makers, Carlton United Breweries in the state of Victoria, made and still make some great flavoured beers like Victoria Bitter, Carlton Draft and Melbourne Bitter. So we drank these other beers and the brewery still laughed all the way to the bank.

For years now I have enjoyed these other beer immensely, especially Victoria Bitter, which we all call VB (VeeBee) or Veebs. If you want to be an authentic Aussie just go into an Aussie pub and ask for a schooner (a three-quarter pint glass) of VB. They'll think you're a local.

In fact, the brewery became my pseudo religion for a time. In Australia we have the Uniting Church of Australia, which was formed when a lot of Methodist, Presbyterian and Congregational Union churches came together to form the third-largest Christian denomination church in Australia. Being a bit of a funny lad in the Army, whenever somebody with rank asked me for my religion I would say "I'm Carlton Uniting Church, Sir!" It was ages before anyone caught on.

One Carlton United lager beer that still earns respect in Australia is Crown Lager. It has an unusual-shaped bottle and a very fancy label. This is a beer we love, but only in the bottle because we look posh when drinking it. Take away the bottle and sales plummet. Carlton United tried selling it on tap a couple of years back but it didn't do well – in blind tasting trials brewers couldn't pick the difference between Crown Lager and other lager beers. So your average bloke holding up the bar at the local pub has no need to hold a glass of expensive beer that tastes like cheap beer.

So, just quietly, it appears we are a lot of secret ale snobs when it comes to packaging but not when it comes to taste.

As a final word of advice, when visiting an Australian home for a barbeque, don't bring a six-pack of Foster's with you. People will just stare, shake their heads and mutter "Another bloody tourist". Bring VB instead, or if you want to impress the Sheilas, bring some Crown Lager.

Either way, Carlton United is still laughing.

Chapter 6: Canned laughter is bad for you

In addition to offering you American guys a few tips about The Land Down Under I reckon it's important that I give you a few examples of how we Aussies view you.

For starters, despite being one of the mightiest countries in the world you Yanks have a few insecurities about you.

One of these is the need for canned laughter on your TV shows.

Now, I am down-right opposed to canned laughter, which you Americans elevated to an art form with the introduction of commercial television and evolved with the recording of sitcoms in front of a live studio audience.

The reason I hate it? It's because having pre-recorded laughter or having studio audiences laugh on-cue pre-supposes that American audiences are too thick in the head to know when they independently recognise something is funny.

I think that is just plain rude. After all, there are no laugh-tracks in Hollywood movies. Think about it, when you are in the cinema you can laugh when you want but TV producers treat you like four-year old children who need to be prompted to laugh on-cue as if you were Pavlov's dog salivating at the ring of a bell.

In my book that kind of sucks and if you believe you are incapable of independent thought then you'll behave accordingly. That's why canned laughter is bad for you.

However, hang on to your hats because I am about to say something that you rarely hear from foreigners: Americans ain't dumb.

"What!" I hear you cry? "No non-American has ever said that about us before????"

Well, to be fair, you Yanks can come off as being somewhat silly to those of us from further afield. Your advertisers and TV producers do treat you like children and there is plenty of proof. We see a lot of American TV around the world and most of it isn't gold-plated brilliance.

I guess what drives this simpleton solution is that there are so damn many of you and there is a commercial desire to round you up like sheep and treat you with the lowest denominator possible just to simplify things.

I mean, with 316 million individual personalities (give or take a few hundred thousand) it is a bit of an advertiser's nightmare to make everyone happy.

But we shouldn't allow simplicity to overshadow the facts of your cleverness. The US is the home of such great inventions like nuclear weapons, Microsoft, Disneyland, Ford Mustangs, Reese's peanut butter cups and pulled-pork sandwiches. I'd hate to live in a world without these wondrous things. I need and respect America.

Being married to an American means I get an outsider's inside view of America, and I can see where the reluctance to unite and rebel against canned laughter comes from.

I suspect it's because you don't think things can be made better because you can be very self-depreciative.

You have a tendency to tear your society apart through criticism because you can – you are the home of free speech, which isn't a bad thing. After all, if you want total conformity go live in North Korea.

Just remind yourself that criticism isn't the end of the story. Acceptance, cooperation, compromise, improvements and unity are the desired outcomes. Come to think of it, that's why they call you the United States.

So I guess what I am saying is cheer up, recognise that you a country of brilliant folk, unite as one people to solve great social issues and most of all say 'NO' to canned laughter.

If America can be the home of the brave then go forward and bravely laugh where no TV producer has laughed before.

You have the smarts to do it.

Chapter 7: Dangerous Creatures

All the Americans I have met seem somewhat hesitant to visit Australia despite their true affection for my native land.

Sure, you all love the idea of immersing yourself into a fantastic adventure in a far-off land populated by friendly locals who will gladly exchange your lucky-bucks for ice-cold beer. However there is one thing that scares you Americans silly but you are too proud to mention it.

So let me point to the elephant in the room and politely say "you are shit-scared of our dangerous creatures".

And to be honest, so you should be. Given half a chance all the wildlife here wants to kill you although perhaps not want to eat you.

I mean, koalas look soft and cuddly but if you happen to come across one in the wild then for goodness' sakes DON'T PICK IT UP. Unless, of course, you want your face to be rearranged by razor-sharp koala claws. Then go right ahead.

You see, our wildlife has a long memory. Just about every wild animal species in Australia was, at some point in our history, hunted and eaten by Aborigines. So just like the Aborigines passing their folklore onto their children so too have the animals passed down through the generations the sage advice that humans are not to be treated as friends. So every last animal in Australia is warned, primed and ready to have a go at you should you give it half a chance.

It doesn't mean you will die a quick and painful death as soon as you get off the Qantas jet in Sydney though. *Au contraire mon ami.*

The key to survival in Australia is to simply leave the animals be. However, accidents do happen and if you should come between a mother Saltwater Crocodile and her eggs you have a choice of two options:

a. Run like hell; or

b. Stand with your feet shoulder-width apart, fold your arms across your chest and die for the Queen.

Personally I recommend Option A but you Americans are awfully brave.

Now there is one thing worse than a tourist being petrified of actual wildlife hazards and that is a tourist being frightened of non-existent Great Southern Monsters. These are the fictional creatures we Aussies have invented to scare the pants off nervous visitors so we can laugh ourselves silly at your expense.

Because I like you Yanks so much I'll tell you about the top three mythical Australian creatures that are sure to be told to you by an evil Aussie 10 minutes after you arrive in The Great Southern Land:

1. Hoop Snakes: A Hoop Snake is a fictional venomous tree snake that feeds on humans and kangaroos. They lie in wait in the branches of tall trees growing on hills. When they spy their prey they gleefully leap into the air and grab their tail with their teeth and hit the ground like an organic hula-hoop, rolling manically down the hill after their prey. The poor mammal cannot hope to move faster than a speeding Hoop Snake and will soon find themselves on the group twitching grotesquely as the snake's venom goes to work. Hoop Snakes are a complete load of crap but the story's effect on children is hilarious to say the least.

2. Drop Bears: These mutant Koalas also live in high trees and live to devour fresh flesh. Sporting massive hairy forearms the Drop Bear will patiently wait for a large mammal (such as a human) to walk/hop under the tree before leaping with a terrifying scream onto its hapless prey, smothering their poor victim with their massive shaggy forearms prior to feasting on raw meat with a side-salad of gum leaves.

3. Bunyips: A Bunyip is a large horrific devil-beast that inhabits creeks and billabongs (small swampy waterways adjacent to rivers) and devours hapless animals and people that wander too close or try to cross the Bunyip's lair. The Bunyip is a part of Aboriginal mythology so be very careful of calling anyone who tells you a Bunyip story a bull-shit artist. If an Aborigine is within earshot of your outburst you'll probably end up with a boomerang in the back of your skull. You have been warned.

Now there is no point in giving you advice on all the dangerous creatures in Australia because there are so many of them. Treat all Australian wildlife as suspicious and you will live longer. However, there are several categories of animals that deserve a special mention:

1. Sharks: Not all sharks in Australian waters want to eat you, but there are plenty who do. So only swim at patrolled beaches because the lifeguards will issue shark warnings. This should be your standard practice anyway because of the dangerous currents on the Australian coast. It is with sad frequency that we hear of tourists drowning on unpatrolled beaches. Please only swim at a beach with life guards.

2. Jellyfish: At the southern beaches you may get stung by a Blue Bottle Jellyfish. These are extremely unpleasant creatures but their sting is usually not dangerous. If they are visiting your beach then jump in your car and move to the next beach. In the far north there are venomous Box

Jellyfish in the water so swallow your pride and swim in a pool. The beaches are still great for strolling along though.

3. Saltwater Crocodiles: These critters live in the far north in salt-water creeks, rivers and the ocean. So don't go in the saltwater up there. Please do not ignore the crocodile warning signs or forget your common sense. Most people who get taken by a crocodile purposely enter unsafe waterways.

4. Snakes: There is no such thing as a cuddly snake in Australia so LEAVE THEM ALONE. If you do something silly though we do have antivenom, therefore if you are going to get bitten then at least have the decency to do it next-door to a hospital.

5. Spiders: The Red Back and Funnel Web spiders rarely cause fatalities anymore because we have developed great antivenom potions. The big black and fuzzy Funnel Web lives in the ground and to be truthful you have to go out of your way to find it. If you do find a spider's nest in the ground then for goodness' sake DON'T STICK YOUR FINGER IN IT. The Red Back likes to live under things like rocks, old tin and old furniture. So don't pick up anything outdoors by its underside unless you have first checked for spiders - it ain't rocket science.

So now that you are all full-bottle on Australian wildlife both real and mythical you have run out of excuses to avoid Australia. Get on the inter-web and book your Qantas Airways ticket now, we'll keep the antivenom fresh and ready for you.

Chapter 8: Why I speak English

Now, it is perfectly OK for an American to say I speak funny. I guess I do.

But among all that funniness is a version of English called Australian. It is more English than American and it is close enough to English for government work. I ought to know, I worked for the Government for over 30 years.

Once upon a time though, not too long ago (in fact it was in the 1960s), for someone to make a career as a reporter or an announcer on the radio or TV in Australia you still had to have what is called a 'clipped BBC accent' - you had to speak the Queen's English. It's no joke: they spoke like they were working for the British Broadcasting Cooperation (BBC). Some people even trained in England to learn the accent properly to get a job back in Australia!

Speaking Australian outside of a pub or the Country Women's Association was deeply frowned upon. However, with the advent of the TV and plenty of American sitcoms with people taking all sorts of funny accents it became allowable for people to speak the Australian lingo in public and in the mass media. Halleluiah and thank you America!

Having studied a few languages myself, I freely admit English is a hard language to 'nut-down' or 'get your head around'. However, it is a very useful language because it is the most widely spoken language in the world according to all the dodgy (unreliable) statistics I have read. And the reason I speak it, in fact the reason I exist, is because of you Yanks.

According to my Mum (Mom), who was around at the time albeit as a child, she reckons the Japs would have invaded Australia during World War 2 and killed off the entire white population and enslaved the rest if they could have got away with it. My Mum is very firm on this, but it isn't well-documented history.

As is happened, the Japs did bomb Australia on numerous occasions (the Imperial Japanese fleet that attacked Pearl Harbour then attacked the city of Darwin in Australia's far north [see Map 3]), and the Japs even attacked Sydney Harbour in 1942 with midget submarines, trying to sink the USS Chicago in the process. Jap subs also sank Allied shipping off the Australian coast, American service personnel died in the defence of Australia and the fear of invasion was very real.

Ultimately for the Japs though, their invasion plans boiled down to a philosophical argument between the Jap Navy and Jap Army because there were too few troops available anyway as they had awakened a sleeping giant called America. This is where you guys come in.

I hope you will think it fair when I regurgitate an old wartime thought about you Americans – "You always turn up late to a World War, but when you do, you put on a splendid show."

Such was the case for Australia.

You see, our best-trained troops were in North Africa and the Middle East fighting the Germans and Italians on Britain's behalf. We had three Army Divisions over there, plus a fourth Division in Malaya and Singapore defending the British Empire's interests. Unfortunately we lost the whole division in Malaya when the Japs invaded. That left the three Divisions on the other side of the planet and no professional forces in Australia.

All we had left in Australia and New Guinea Army-wise were militia and home-service battalions who were patriotic, dedicated and training hard to face any invasion but they needed time and equipment to prepare for war. We needed you Yanks badly and, for the love of God, you did not let us down.

US Army Air Corps pilots, alongside our own Royal Australian Air Force, threw themselves at the enemy over Australia and New Guinea. Our navies fought as integrated Task Forces, fighting and dying together at sea, while our troops fought it out in the southwest Pacific jungles, destroying any chance the Japs had of executing the young Miss Horan (who turned out to be my Mum).

The rest, as they say, is history, and it is the reason an English-speaking Australia survived the war.

Now I am not gilding the lily. In fact, our famous wartime Prime Minister Mr John Curtain made the switch from Britain to the US official when his New Year message for 1942 was printed in the papers in late December 1941:

"'Without any inhibitions of any kind, I make it clear that Australia looks to America, free of any pangs as to our traditional links or kinship with the United Kingdom."

Of course this pissed-off British Prime Minister Winston Churchill a fair bit and was of concern to US President Franklin D. Roosevelt because it meant you Yanks now had another allied partner to bail out.

But it was a brave move by our PM – he put the nation's security ahead of Imperial sensitivities, and in doing so set the course that Australia continues to follow to this day, and it is the reason I am still allowed to speak English.

This is because ever since 1942 Australia's national security has been underwritten by America.

It's no joke. In fact in the centre of Russell Offices (our version of the Pentagon) there is a great-big-bloody-tall monument to the Americans at the epicentre of our military's nerve centre.

The Australian-American Memorial is topped by an American bald eagle with its wings thrown so high it looks like Bugs Bunny (that's its nickname). Nowadays many Australians think it was paid for by our Government, but it was, in fact, paid for by public subscription after the war.

And it was over-subscribed. This really speaks volumes about what we think about you Americans.

It the following decades we have fought alongside Americans in Korea, Vietnam, Iraq and Afghanistan and we have served on numerous humanitarian aid and peacekeeping missions together. We train so closely that we don't even blink when we see an American uniform – it's all run-of-the-mill even though you guys are from the opposite side of the world.

Joining with our Kiwi cousins (i.e. New Zealanders), the Australia, New Zealand and United States Security (ANZUS) Treaty is the most important security relationship imaginable to us. If one of us is ever attacked the other two will come to the other's aid. We even enacted the treaty on September 11, 2001, when our Prime Minister, who was in Washington DC that day, ordered the Royal Australian Air Force fighter aircraft and pilots training in the US to immediately deploy with their US Air Force counterparts to patrol the skies of America.

So the next time you see an Aussie on your TV or taking the place of an American in a Hollywood movie, don't write him or her off as a funny-sounding foreigner pinching Yankee lucky-bucks.

They are just representatives of a very grateful nation trying to earn some Benjamins to pay their mortgage with.

God bless you America. Keep on sharing your dollars and please come and visit us.

Chapter 9: Speaking Strail-yun

The key to survival in any new environment is to be able to communicate with the locals. Get it right and you will be treated like royalty. Get it wrong and you'll be left out in the cold like kangaroo pooh in the snow.

Now you Yanks probably think we Australians talk an alien language focused on beer, Sheilas, Blokes, more beer, barbeques and cricket. While that is technically correct we do speak a variation of the Queen's English which you can quite easily get your head around with a few tips from me.

For starters, don't be afraid to ask us to speak a bit slower while you get up to speed with how we talk. Having lived overseas with Europeans who speak better English than I do, which really hurts when you consider it is a second language for them, I have learnt that talking through your nose at the speed of sound does not make for polite multinational dinner conversation. So as you come to terms with our accent and colloquial terminology it is perfectly fine to ask us to speak slower. We will still think you are an idiot but we will comply.

The next bit is the tricky bit. We Aussies take dry sarcasm and irony to extremes. So not everything we say is quite heart-felt and sincere. In fact, most of the time we are taking the piss out of you (i.e. we are taking the Mickey out of you).

So if we tell you your opinion is "the best idea since canned beer" you should be on your guard as we are being sarcastic. What we are really saying is "Your idea has no merits whatsoever and your mouth should be sewn shut."

Or if you were to ask "Will I see kangaroos on the streets of Sydney?" we might just reply "Sure, if you drink enough beer first."

Irony is a bit tougher for Americans to understand and we Aussies are masters at it. For example, in Australia every redheaded man is called Blue, a short man is called Lofty and even crocodiles have been referred to as 'long-nosed long-tailed short-legged terriers'. Even my Mum calls our Queen "Betty Windsor, housewife-extraordinaire". There's no end to our cleverness.

You may even call your best mate a 'total bastard' while a real total bastard is called 'a bit of a bastard'. However this can backfire quite easily if you don't have the inflection right so don't try it until you have first lived in Australia for 50 years or have drunk 10,000 schooners of Victorian Bitter, whichever comes first (probably the second option, it's part of the express-processing requirements for Australian citizenship).

The next part is common to learning any foreign language and that is learning the vernacular. The following vocabulary list is not exhaustive and in no particular order but will set you up for a measure of success against us devilishly-humorous Australians:

Strail-ya: Australians can't pronounce the word 'Australia' as it won't fit through the nose. So we say 'Strail-ya'. Try saying it through your nose; it gives you a pleasant tingling sensation on the rims of your nostrils.

Drongo: A Drongo is a colloquial name for a loser or a no-hoper. The name comes from an Australian 1920's racehorse which, despite good form and a good heart, never won a race from 37 starts. It did pay for itself with five second placing's and seven third placing's, so Drongo was always a favourite of the public who tried to will it to win. Alas, in the end Drongo was there to make up the numbers. So if someone calls you a Drongo you're the champion that never was. Try to avoid it.

A few kangaroos loose in the top paddock: 'To be mad, crazy'. Chances are you have things going on in your brain that shouldn't be revealed in polite company. Curb your desire to talk about your assault weapon collection – we don't like crazy people.

She'll be right: Stupid Australian optimism; we always say "She'll be right' even as the car plummets over the 300-foot cliff into the raging river below.

Strewth: 'My Goodness that surprises me!'

Your shout: Be very careful with this one, your life hangs in the balance. In Australia at the pub it is customary for a group of mates to buy a round of drinks in turn. Should you refuse to buy your round, called a 'shout' (so called because you have to shout your order to the barmaid in order to be heard over the voices of the 2,000 other Blokes trying to order a beer), you will be summarily executed. If you leave the bar before it is your shout and neglect to buy a shout for those remaining you will be tracked down and summarily executed.

Stuffed: This one is tricky as it has a variety of meanings. To say "I'm stuffed' could mean you are full of food, tired or you have had it and are about to die. 'Get Stuffed' is the equivalent of telling someone to stick something where the sun doesn't shine.

Pig's arse: 'I am sorry, I don't agree with your last comment.'

Fair dinkum: As a question is means 'are you/is it for real?' As a statement of fact it means 'I am being very truthful'. It can also be used to endorse something as being the real thing. For example, there is no greater accolade than to be called a 'Fair Dinkum Aussie'.

Ute: An Australian car with a flatbed tray on the back (i.e. a utility car). It comes from the idea that a farmer should be able to drive a work vehicle around the farm from Monday to Saturday and still drive it to church on a Sunday without looking crass. It has ordinary car seats in the front and is definitely not a truck. We have been building theses since the 1930s and they are really popular here. I am told you Yanks have built Utes in the past such as the Chevrolet El Camino and the Ford Ranchero but these were laughed out of existence.

Stone the crows: See Strewth.

Dunny: A toilet, more specifically an outhouse. Regardless of the location, if someone announces they are going to the dunny you know they are headed to the smallest room to relieve themselves.

A Furphy: A rumour or tall story that is claimed to be a fact but disbelieved by others. It originates from the small horse-drawn water carts manufactured by J. Furphy and Sons in Victoria. The carts were iconic and widely used. Workers would gather around one for a drink and swap gossip, hence when someone hears a story they don't believe they say "Aw, that's a Furphy, Mate!"

Crikey: See Strewth.

Fair Go: Australia is a very equal-minded society as the original British settlers were the dregs of British society. This meant there has been no room in Australia for a class system, unlike in Britain. As such it is a national trait that everyone is given a fair go at every given opportunity. Australians can grow up to be anything they want – poor, rich, famous or a recluse. There is only one thing an ordinary Australian can't do and that is move within the circles of people from families with old money (i.e. the old established rich families). The doors are firmly shut there and I think the same applies in America.

No worries mate: "Everything is good" or "I know what I am doing", i.e. famous last words.

Up at sparrow's fart: To be up and about at dawn.

Bangers: Colloquial word for sausages, so named because until recent years sausages had so much fat in them they would burst apart if you did not first prick them to let the hot liquid fat escape. It's not a problem now, our bangers are much healthier but we still use the name.

Bottlo: The bottle shop, the shop dedicated to selling booze. I've seen them in America under different names, however the function is the same.

Crook: Can mean a thief or to feel ill. i.e. "Crikey I feel crook!" To be 'As crook as Rookwood' means you are very ill – Rookwood is the necropolis in western Sydney, a place you definitely don't want to end up in.

Dag: Someone with poor dress sense, e.g. "He's a real dag". Named after the bits of pooh that stick to a sheep's bum, it's not a compliment.

Pissed off: To be really annoyed as you have been treated like a piece of pooh stuck to the toilet bowl which has been hosed-off with urine. Please, don't piss off an Aussie; however we do say it a lot.

Smoko: Morning tea, except we don't usually smoke a cigarette with it anymore.

Up shit creek: To be in a spot of bother.

Wanker: Someone who is full of themselves, it comes from the term to please yourself with your hand. On no accounts give anyone a reason to call you a wanker.

Schooner: A common beer drinking glass used in pubs. It is a bit smaller than a pint.

Victoria Bitter: A common Australian beer that is a good all-rounder and the complete opposite of Coors.

Chapter 10: You can't polish an American Turd

Having got this far I reckon we have built up a bit of trust, so it's time to let you in on another fact-of-Australian-life opinion when it comes to the US.

You see, not everything you guys do is gold-plated brilliance. Some of it stinks like a bag of prawn heads in the sun.

Just because you chaps are awfully good at advertising doesn't mean you can use smoke and mirrors to disguise something that should never have seen the light of day.

So to put it in Australian words "you can't polish an American turd".

Take for example your home shopping channels on the TV which you have unfortunately exported. No amount of advertising using yesterday's TV celebrities is going to make me buy a 'Huge-Abs-O-Matic' machine. It just doesn't add up to me. If a piece of amazingly cheap twisty mechanised under-bed-storage fitness equipment was so fantastic at giving me the abdominal muscles of a Greek God then I would have been issued one at birth along with my silver spoon (I never got one of those either).

Likewise not every Hollywood movie is fit for consumption. Take for example Sex and the City: The Movie. While it might be considered a cult-classic by the Sheilas I can tell you it should be tried for crimes against the men of mankind. After sitting through this movie in a bid to show female empathy I am now of the belief that if I want to get in touch with my feminine side I will shake hands with my wife.

Probably the worst turd in the American paddock though belongs to the most sacred of artefacts, that being beer. I came along this American brontosaurus-size turd in, of all places, Scotland while studying at university.

You see, in the 1990s I had knee injuries from being an Army paratrooper. I had switched from the Regular Army (full-time) to the Army Reserve (part-time) due to the career-halting injury and had taken on a rather boring job for a year as an administrator with a Defence contractor while my knees were seen to by a doctor paid for by Veteran Affairs.

It was during this time that I learnt that I had created my own glass ceiling for career progression outside of the Army by not finishing high school. So with plenty of British pluck I enrolled as a mature-age student at a not-so-glamorous Sydney-based university to study journalism.

During my first year I also studied philosophy and enjoyed it so much that I seriously thought of changing my degree program to ponder the great thoughts on the meaning life and the universe. These thoughts soon disappeared when I realised if I wanted to be able to earn enough money to pay for food then I'd better study something that actually paid a wage.

So it was back to journalism and in my second year I spent a semester at Napier University in Edinburgh, Scotland, studying journalism and video production. Being in the Australian Army Reserve I was also able to do exchange service with a local British Territorial Army (now called the British Army Reserve) unit full of guys my age and with my attitude.

Anyhow, being a mature-age student meant that I was turning 31 when most of my fellow university students were turning 21 (note that in Australia and Great Britain the legal drinking age is 18 years old). One night we students gathered for a pint at a local pub and it was politely pointed out that they served Australian Foster's Lager beer on-tap. I was asked if I would like a pint of Foster's to cure any homesickness.

After telling my fellow students never to say anything so stupid to me again they then invited me to try a pint of Coors beer. Although it was American beer it was very cheap and my younger friends were a bit strapped for cash and so they often drank Coors to make their British pennies go farther. Against my better judgement I decided to show solidarity with my poor brethren and ordered a Coors.

All it took was one sip to know I had tasted an American turd. Coors is so damned awful that it was the first and only beer that I have never finished. Think about it: how bad does a beer have to be to turn an Aussie off his birthright?

So while the other students drank Coors I drank hearty Scottish real ale beers for the night. I noticed that the other students were trying to keep up with me so I warned them that they should on no account do so. After all, I was a mature-age Australian soldier who could drink them under the table – words that would come back to haunt me.

This is because they were still young – they still had their drinking training wheels on. Things are a bit different once they become fully-grown Scottish drinking monsters.

I can still recall one evening spent on the drink with my Scottish army buddies. I was on my 10th pint and still standing with the help of the bar, albeit only just. I was pretty pleased with myself when I noticed one of my haggis-munching mates put down his empty 12th pint glass and wink at me and say: "Och Cameron, yer slowing down laddie!"

Such is humility. However I am pleased to say that since those dark days of the 1990s you Yanks have really changed your ways. Your micro-brewed beer is phenomenal, and if I was asked to say what was my favourite massed-produced beer in the world I would look you in the eye and confidently say "Alaskan Amber". I think it is wonderful that you Americans have rebelled against mass-produced drudgery and have embraced your tastebuds. It just goes to prove that Americans are ultimately not satisfied with mega-manufactured rubbish.

Anyway, getting back to the subject, I would like to summarise this chapter with a few points:

1. You can't polish an American turd;

2. Never try to out-drink a Scotsman; and

3. Never drink Coors beer. I may have done some stupid things in my life but I am not dumb enough to try a second Coors.

Chapter 11: Talking Dogs

Just like you Americans, we Aussies love our pets. Not that we have the Texan fetish for keeping Asian Tigers as conversation pieces, but when it comes to domestic pets we would seem to be on par with you Yanks.

Except for one small detail: You see, we Aussies know how to talk with our dogs.

After all, we are a nation famous for our working dogs and quite frankly it's not too hard to do. You just need to have your smarts about you.

For starters, a poor dog doesn't have lips and so can't make vowel sounds. This means elocution lessons are wasted on a canine, and if you're expecting to have a philosophical discussion with your mutt about why cats should be concentrated on a remote Pacific island that is scheduled for nuclear demolition you should perhaps engage instead in conversation with a talking Sulphur Crested Cockatoo (an Australian native bird). At least it will acknowledge your existence with repeated requests for crackers.

However, if you understand that a dog has ears, has probably grown up listening to English or Amglish (American English) every day in your household then it is very likely that after a couple of years the basics of human language is bound to have set into your best friend's brain.

So the first thing to accept is that dogs understand English. When you also consider that a dog is permanently stuck in adolescence then you also understand why they have selective hearing. They aren't stupid, they are just being teenagers. When they take a wiz on the carpet they are not ignoring your toilet training. They are just testing the boundaries of your authority and patience as any good teenager would do.

The other key point to understand is that while a dog can't form words with its mouth it can communicate with facial expressions - especially with its eyes and brow.

So when you are eating dinner and the dog is intently watching you he not just saying "Can I have some?" What he is really saying is "Give me your food if you value the sanctity of the living room rug". It's not rocket science.

Take for example my dog Darwin the Beagle. He is a lovely chap that I chose as a puppy before his eyes first opened. He is named for the naturalist Sir Charles Darwin, the man who reckoned we were more akin to monkeys than miracles. He visited Australia on HMS Beagle during the ship's famous second voyage, which later resulted in the naming of the City of Darwin, which looks out onto Beagle Gulf, in the Northern Territory. It is all terribly fascinating stuff and highly suitable for giving a dog a silly name.

Anyway, my dog Darwin grew up with me and has been my faithful companion ever since I brought him home. He has heard more English than Doglish, so seeing as he can communicate with other dogs it also follows that he must at least understand the basics of English. After all, when I say to him "Do you want a treat?" his eyes light up. When I say "Want to help me wash the dishes?" he doesn't show the slightest interest.

So there you go. I may not win a Nobel Prize for animal welfare but I reckon my science stacks up, and if you know how to read a dog's face then you can have some cracking conversations.

Take for example the conversation we had the other day in the garden. I was bent-over weeding and he was patrolling the front fence when a newspaper sailed over the fence and landed with a 'whump' on the lawn.

I watched him walk over to the newspaper, sniff it and then, after turning up his nose at it, he calmly turned and walked away.

I called out to him "What's up boy, don't you like the news today?" This stopped him in his tracks and he turned and looked at me as if I was the biggest idiot in the world.

"It's the local paper you moron," he said with his eyes. "Even you don't read that rubbish."

Then there was the rather frank discussion we had on the touchy subject of S-E-X. After a rather wonderful afternoon spent at home in the bedroom with my wife in a rare child-free domestic environment I staggered out to the kitchen for a much needed glass of water to find Darwin spread out mournfully on the kitchen tiles looking like someone had eaten the last pancake without sharing it with him (I have seen this disgust before).

His expression and posture stopped me in my tracks. "What's wrong?" I cried out to my Beagle.

He lifted his sad face towards me and said "Look, it's all right for you, you have a spouse who lives here. I live behind fences without any female company. It all makes for a rather terrible love-life."

I was shocked and saddened to hear this from my dog. It made me feel like a bad parent.

"I am so sorry to hear that, I never really thought about your needs properly," I said. "Would it help if I let you out for a bit of a stroll a couple of evenings a week to meet the local lasses?"

"That would be splendid," he replied.

I said "Is there anything else I can do for you?"

Darwin paused, glanced at his loins and then looked me straight in the face.

"Do you mind if I borrow your balls?" he asked.

"You see, mine went missing that first time you took me to the Vet."

Chapter 12: Working for the Queen

I am a bloke who has worked for the ultimate Sheila all my working life and I am bloody proud of it.

I joined the Army as a common soldier at age 17 under the reign of Elizabeth the Second, by the Grace of God Queen of Australia and Her other Realms and Territories, Head of the Commonwealth. 30 years later I was an Australian Army officer holding the Queen's commission. I absolutely loved it but I will understand if you think my royal affection means I am a bit nuts.

With a title like hers you might expect Her Majesty to be a bit of a snob, but she's far from it. Also the Queen of 15 other Commonwealth countries, Queen Elizabeth II provides quite the counterpoint to the US President. The reason I bring this up is because I know you Yanks are rather curious about why we have retained the British monarch long after you gave UK royalty a great big boot in the bum.

The key thing to understand about a constitutional monarchy is that it is very different to having a president. In your case the President is the head of state, head of government, leader of the executive branch of the US and the Commander-in-Chief of the Defense Forces. That's a lot of power invested in one person.

This came about because since 1776 you have gone out of your way to make sure your government looked nothing like a monarchy. As a result you did what you have always done since – come up with the most complicated and convoluted way of doing something to prove you are not British.

Not that I'm complaining, after all politics and government is a dirty game anywhere on the globe. So I am not out to trash your system of government. Hopefully though, I might be able to show you a few good points about having a Queen for you to mull over.

For starters, the Queen, through her appointed Australian Governor-General, provides a symbolic and oversight role rather than wield executive power. The Queen embodies the legality and legitimate authority under which our Government and its departments operate. Likewise, the Queen, through the Governor-General, provides advice to the Government of the day and undertakes the oversight duties for the parliamentary processes and the leadership of the day.

This is why our national leader, called the Prime Minister, needs to do a good job, because the Governor-General can sack a Prime Minister who doesn't have the confidence of the House of Representatives, and believe me, we sacked one Prime Minister in the 1970s for just such a reason – I bet you Yanks would just love that option, right?

So we have a fail-safe oversight mechanism to monitor our national leader. Unfortunately for you Americans, in your Government the top-dog has no higher-ranked oversight person. So there's no-one to preside over the President, instead there's just a bureaucratic jungle. Cheer up though, the Russians are just as bad and do the same sort of thing, however they have a firing squad to ensure politicians comply with their President.

Now in some countries their president does the work of the Queen. That is, they provide the overwatch for the government and let the Prime Minister run things. Unfortunately you guys don't have a Prime Minister so you are right-royally screwed.

I reckon you are probably starting to giggle and protest that we don't have an Australian citizen as our top-most leader. Well, I don't know if the Queen has an Australian passport (how would you like to be the border protection guy who asks for it when she pops into Sydney?) but her face is on the reverse of all our coins so at least I guess everyone knows her. That should make her a bit of an Aussie.

Anyway, while the Governor-General is appointed by the Queen she makes her decision on who gets the G-G job based on the recommendation of the Australian Government of the day. In recent decades we have had some of Australia's greatest leaders who were not previously politicians assigned to the top position. Just think, our appointed local overseer is not a corrupted and jaded politician. This is the gift that just keeps giving.

Another ridiculously good reason to keep the Queen is because she works for free! Australians do not pay her a wage or pay an allowance for her residences outside of Australia. We only pay the bill when she is in Australia or acting solely as the Queen of Australia. We do pay, quite rightly, for the Governor General's upkeep and wages and also for the various state governors who perform the same function at the state level. That's fair enough because they live and work here.

When you think about how much it costs for the upkeep of the US President, including the Presidential jet and supporting aircraft, you'll see that we Aussies are laughing all the way to the bank. For goodness sake, Her Majesty even flies to Australia commercially on British Airways! What a woman…

Anyway, I bet your just chaffing at the bit to tell me that the Queen is out of touch with the common people. While that has been arguably true for centuries of British monarchs, I think you could say this woman and her father have sacrificed everything for their royal roles.

Take the Queen's father, Prince Albert who became King George VI. Being the second son of King George V he was not expected to succeed to the throne as his elder brother Edward was fitted-up for that job.

Albert served happily in the Royal Navy and even saw active service in World War 1, which makes him a champ in my eyes. Happily married to his soul mate with two beautiful daughters, he was the ultimate family man who was deeply relieved that he wouldn't be king. Things changed though when his brother Edward decided to marry an American divorcée (which, funnily enough, I did too).

Edward became King Edward VIII upon the death of his father in 1936 but when he next announced that he wanted to marry American socialite and multiple divorcée Wallis Simpson the British parliament went ape and said 'NO' very loudly because it would upset the church and set a bad example for the politicians (who evidently had never had affairs with showgirls).

So Edward abdicated and Albert became King George VI and was a smash hit. When the Nazis threatened to invade his homeland during World War 2, did the King run away to Canada as he was advised to do by senior officials? No sir, he stayed put and put up with the bombings along with the rest of Britain. He and his family were a shining beacon of light and hope in an evil pitch blackness. Even the King's daughter Elizabeth, now our Queen, joined the Women's Auxiliary Territorial Service and trained as a military driver and mechanic once she was old enough.

Unfortunately for the King the pressures of doing a superb job of a job he never wanted led to his premature death in 1952 from a blood clot to the heart, brought on in part through his increased dependence on cigarettes to carry on with his royal duties. Australia had lost its greatest King but gained its greatest Queen.

"But", I hear you cry, "The Queen lives a life of riches and comfort. And, most of all, she isn't elected to the position. Isn't that unfair and undemocratic?"

I'm glad you asked.

Well, I guess she has never had to use newspaper as toilet paper and her castles are rather large and beyond my price-range but she does do a job you wouldn't want for quids (i.e. there isn't enough money in the world to convince me), even if you could be elected to the position.

Take for example all those boring banquets, interpretive cultural dances and long-winded speeches she has had to sit through for six decades. A lesser mortal would slit their own wrists after a week. She is surrounded by politicians and politics, yet has never accidently shot herself.

Also consider that she has very little private life as she is surrounded by so many staff, her life is constantly in danger from psycho-murderers and terrorists plus everything her and her family does ends up in the Media. The benefits might be good but the job description really sucks.

Finally, consider the value of having a leader who was raised to rule. Queen Elizabeth has known since her uncle sold his soul to an American that one day the top job would be hers. She didn't need to plot and make drug deals to get into power. Instead she was able to focus on her duties and responsibilities without the political shenanigans.

The same goes for her children, grandchildren and great-grandchildren. They know what is coming and they spend their lives learning how to be worthy and execute their various solemn Royal duties. I would much rather have a member of the Royal Family be my monarch than trust a questionable career politician with the country's ultimate power any day of the week.

Our Queen inherited a job that she didn't want and it is the same job that killed her father. Yet she has remained true to the vow she made over 60 years ago when she became Queen:

"I declare before you all that my whole life, whether it be long or short, shall be devoted to your service and the service of our great imperial family to which we all belong."

Take it from me; our lady is one hell of a lady.

Chapter 13: Anthem Madness

Just to prove we are a real country we do have a National Anthem. Unfortunately it has only been in my lifetime that we have sung a song about Australia. Let me explain.

You may recall that a key reason for the British occupying The Great Southern Land was because they suddenly found themselves America-less. This proved to be a spot of bother because besides wanting a place to banish their untidy convicts the Brits also naturally needed another land to exploit and make a bit of coin out of.

Now, what I am about to tell you was once considered very Top Secret and hush-hush, so don't tell anyone.

The Brits thought they had found a source of a significant strategic material on an island off the Australian east coast. This material was so important and rare that it sealed the British decision to set up a mainland colony in Sydney on the edge of the known world.

What was this amazing strategic material?

It was ship's mast timbers.

No, I am not joking - think about the technology of the time. Near Australia's east coast on Norfolk Island there were growing Norfolk Pines (we don't waste time dreaming up flowery names for trees in Australia). Anyway, while Britain ruled the seas through the superior Royal Navy and hence ruled the trade routes, there was a major glitch that threatened to undermine their naval superiority.

While Britain still had supplies of hardwood such as oak to support its shipbuilding industry, there was a slight problem when it came to ship's masts. You see, they had unfortunately exhausted their supplies of tall straight softwood trees in the 1600s. That was okay though because they had stumbled across a great supply of White Pines (another example of non-effort tree naming) in Britain's North America colonies. That was good for 125 years but your bastards ended up shutting down that supply.

The main alternative was found in the Baltic States and came from Baltic Pine trees (does anyone put any effort into naming trees?). Now getting hold of these incredibly important, solid, flexible, tall and straight timbers was problematic as there were rather expensive and the Baltic States were fickle about whom they were allied with at any given time and to whom they would sell their precious pine logs to.

It also caused a balance-of-payment problem as the masts cost more than the goods the Brits sold to the Baltic countries in return, which meant handing over government gold. So the Brits had a dilemma, and you don't have to be a genius to work out that a sailing warship without masts is a bugger of a boat to paddle, even with the best of British pluck.

So having access to your own supply of ship's masts supplies was absolutely worth the bother of the trip to the Land Down Under.

If you don't believe me consider the fact that the first thing the Brits did after the First Fleet arrived in the Sydney region in 1788 was to send a ship with a small number of troops, free settlers and convicts to prepare Norfolk Island for development. Eventually Norfolk Island became infamous for its hellish treatment of convicts.

Unfortunately the Norfolk Pines turned out to be rubbish. You see, British naval explorers had earlier reported the presence of pine trees on Norfolk Island as they sailed by but had neglected to land and try one out. Once they got there and cut one down it was discovered the trees rot from the inside-out as they grow and were not structurally sound for ship's masts. What a bummer.

Anyhow, Norfolk Island was still used on and off for a while as a penal colony but it fizzled out, only to be reinhabited by descendants of the mutiny on the Bounty blokes and their Tahitian Sheilas. Isn't history wonderful?

So what does all this have to do with our national anthem? Bugger-all I guess (i.e. probably nothing), but it make for a good yarn (story).

Oh yes, it also means that from 1788 until 1974 we were stuck with the Brit's 'God Save the Queen/King' as our national anthem.

While I am a royalist and I do admire the Queen, this anthem does lack a bit of homage to Australia:

God save our gracious Queen
Long live our noble Queen
God save the Queen
Send her victorious
Happy and glorious
Long to reign over us
God save the Queen

You see, it mentions the monarch a fair bit but excludes the poor folk who do the manual work, even in the five verses that follow. Mind you, it has many uses for music die-hards. For example, substitute 'Bon Jovi' for 'Queen' in the song, change 'her' to 'them' and you have a fan club hymn.

It was only during my time as a child that the Australian Government started work on getting popular support for a national anthem that actually had Australia in the lyrics.

In 1974 the Prime Minister declared 'Advance Australia Fair' would be the national anthem, while on Royal occasions 'God Save the Queen' would also be played. Not bad thinking for the time.

This was undone soon after by the next Prime Minister and it wasn't until 1984 when our Governor-General finally issued a definitive proclamation that 'God Save the Queen' was the designated Royal Anthem, to be played at events attended by the Royal family, and 'Advance Australia Fair' would finally be the true Australian national anthem. It's a bonzer song and the first verse goes like this:

Australians all let us rejoice
For we are young and free
We've golden soil and wealth for toil
Our home is girt by sea
Our land abounds in nature's gifts
Of beauty rich and rare
In history's page, let every stage
Advance Australia Fair

Actually, it brings a tear to my eye just to type it, and what's even better is that it only has two verses. What is absolutely fantastic is that the entire nation doesn't even know most of the second verse. So on those rare occasions when we have to sing the second verse we just sing the second verse's first line – 'Beneath our radiant Southern Cross' – and then mumble the rest. It works every time.

Now, a close contender for Aussie national anthem was 'Waltzing Matilda', which when you think about it is incredibly dumb because it is a song about the world's worst sheep thief. Here are some of the lyrics with my translations inserted:

Once a jolly swagman (an itinerant worker travelling on foot wearing a hat with corks hanging off it) *camped by a billabong* (a small swamp)

Under the shade of a coolabah tree (finally, a flowery-name for a tree! It's a native Eucalyptus tree that grows next to billabongs)

And he sang as he watched and waited 'till his billy boiled (he boiled his camping kettle to make another cup of crappy tea)

"Who'll come a-waltzing Matilda with me?" (Who will join the Swaggie in walking along with a bed-roll containing your worldly goods without much joy?)

Down came a jumbuck (a bloody great big male sheep) *to drink at the billabong*

Up jumped the swagman and grabbed him with glee

And he sang as he shoved that jumbuck in his tucker bag (i.e. he stole and killed the sheep to cut it up and put in his food bag):

"You'll come a-waltzing Matilda with me" (as if the dead sheep had a choice)

Up rode the squatter mounted on his thoroughbred (along came the farmer who paid nothing for his land riding a rather expensive and show-off horse)

Down came the troopers, one, two, and three (along came three cops on much cheaper horses)

"Whose is that jolly jumbuck you've got in your tucker bag? (i.e. we reckon you stole this farmer's sheep you homeless bum)

"You'll come a-waltzing Matilda with me" (i.e. it's off to jail for you sunshine)

Up jumped the swagman and sprang into the billabong.
"You'll never take me alive!" said he (the silly bastard drowned himself over one tasty sheep)
And his ghost may be heard as you pass by that billabong:
"Who'll come a-waltzing Matilda with me?"

So ultimately there were, and still are, a bunch of Australian rednecks that want a song about the world's stupidest sheep thief to be our national anthem.

You Americans aren't the only population with crazy people.

Chapter 14: Sharing the Wealth

I keep banging-on about how import America's support and security umbrella is to making Australia a free and happy nation. I do this because it is true, honourable and deserves recognition.

We do, however, keep good ties with the old mother-country and not just through our noble Queen. In fact, we are still a member of a very grand club once known as the British Empire, then the British Commonwealth and now the Commonwealth of Nations.

They used to say that the sun never sets on British Empire because it was always day-time somewhere in the Empire. The same thing could almost be said about the Commonwealth of Nations because it is so flaming huge.

How's this for eye-popping statistics: The Commonwealth consists of 53 nations spanning all six continents, covering nearly a quarter of the earth's landmass and represents nearly a third of the world's population. More to the point, there's not a blessed Yankee anywhere to be seen.

Now, as my father used to say to me, "If you want to run with the big dogs then you have to piss further up the post". So Australia has to pull its weight within this huge cooperative and we do rise to the occasion. We have strong military ties with our Commonwealth partners (some more than others), we wrestle with the others in the Commonwealth's economic forum and we absolutely uphold the group's stance on human rights.

This last point is important because the Commonwealth has a lot of high-level ideas. For example, here are human-speak translations of some of its lofty and flowery-worded principles and values:

a. International peace and the rule of international law are bloody good ideas;

b. Equal rights for every individual Bloke and Sheila;

c. The eradication of poverty, ignorance, disease and economic inequality would be the best thing since sliced bread;

d. Racial prejudice and discrimination are nasty so don't do these things; and

e. Economic and social development is something we must get our head around and work hard at so that people can live happily ever after.

All in all these are grand ideas and it is to our credit that these are being pursued as a collective. Come to think of it, when you compare it to the US constitution it seems to read like we have our own United States of everyone-who-doesn't-want-to-be-American. I think it's pretty nifty just quietly.

Now within this great big Commonwealth there are naturally some nations whose relationship with Australia is a little bit more equal than others. For starters there is New Zealand, that tiny country to the east of Australia where they spend an awful lot of effort trying to be more British than the British. They have a lovely country that unfortunately sits on the fault line of adjoining tectonic plates, which means they are prone to earthquakes.

The Kiwis, as we like to call them (after their native flightless bird that is also a national symbol), are our best mates and are akin to being your favourite cousins who always drop in to watch sport on your TV and drink all the beer in your fridge. We love them, most of them live in Australia but they always retain their own funny accent (yes, I know that's the pot calling the kettle 'black') and we have shed blood together on many a battlefield. Doubtless we will continue to do so.

Then there are the Brits themselves. We call the English the 'Poms', after the French word for apples, because we reckon they are a bunch of apple-munching pale-skinned folk from the opposite side of the planet who all secretly crave to move to Australia because we have that strange commodity called sunlight. Australia is full of Poms as well as Scots, Northern Irish and the odd Welsh-person. They are like the cousins who live a bit further away and who always seem to have a runny nose.

I guess the Canadians are a lot like us (except for the French-Canadians: they are a lot like no-one else on the planet). They have a similar sense of humour and we love them too but they are like the cousins who live too far away and we don't see enough of them. They are the reason we need supersonic trans-Pacific airliners – so we can hang out and listen to them tell hilarious stories about French Canadians.

There are plenty of Asian and African member nations in the Commonwealth too, plus India and Pakistan bring a lot of people to the party despite their near obsession with destroying one another (just look at their post-British Empire history of playing nicely together – it makes for the world's thinnest book). So it's a very diverse club that helps balance Australia's place in the world – we are not solely aligned with America to our northeast.

Australia is globally linked-in through the Commonwealth and other bilateral relationships. Without being rude I think this is a cracking idea because it means there is no need for Australia to be the 51st US state or for me to have to give up my outrageous accent to sound mid-western.

So sharing some of our wealth with the Commonwealth works well for us. Mind you, I wouldn't want to rely on any of them if someone threatened to attack Australia. You Yanks are the 1,000-pound gorilla in the room that stops people throwing punches at us. Thank God for America, long may you be our 'Gorilla Commonwealth'.

Chapter 15: Identity Crisis

While we Aussies genuinely admire you Yanks there is something about your collective persona that baffles us, and indeed the rest of the world.

You see, if I may be so bold as to say, we do believe you lot seem to have a bit of an identity crisis.

What I mean is that many of you Yanks aren't happy being labelled solely as an American. You always have to qualify it.

For example, we regularly hear Americans call themselves an African-American, Irish-American, German-American, Hispanic American and so on.

What's wrong with being plain-old American? After all, you come from the land of the brave and the free. You are the might that puts the right into the right to be free.

That's a pretty awesome label, don't you think? I would have thought you would be as proud as punch to call yourself a Yankee-Doodle fully-paid-up and solid-to-the-core American.

So what is it with you Yanks?

Over here in The Great Southern Land we are happy as a kid with a box of donuts and not an adult in sight to be called Aussies. We love being Australians, it's the duck's-guts, it is a badge of honour and a ticket to our birth-right to drink beer by the gallon and to barbeque meat like there's no tomorrow.

You, on the other hand, clearly have an identity problem that runs deep. Let me give you an example of the worst US identity crisis I have ever witnessed.

Some years ago I was deployed as a soldier to Camp Victory in Baghdad, Iraq, as part of the coalition headquarters forces based near Baghdad International Airport.

There were thousands of people based there and all coalition nationalities would eat at the US-run Dining Facility, which served pretty good Yankee-style food. In fact it was so good it was like being in America except more people were trying to kill me – Baghdad is like that.

Anyway, I was sitting down to my gourmet US-made highly-processed pulled-pork oh-my-God-you-taste-fantastic sandwich when two US soldiers sat next to me and started chatting away. Being Americans they were rather loud (well, you are loud so don't blame me) and I heard the bloke next to me say the following:

"Well, as for myself, I am Welsh-American."

This, dear reader, pushed me over the edge and for the sake of sanity I felt compelled to intervene. After all, a Welsh-American? Talk about your minorities.

"Excuse me," I interjected. "Did you just describe yourself as Welsh-American?"

"Yes sir," said the soldier.

The conversation then ran like this:

"Were you born in America?"

"Yes sir."

"Were your parents born in America?"

"Yes sir."

"Were your grandparents all born in America?"

"Yes sir."

"Then for the love of God YOU ARE AN AMERICAN!"

He wouldn't speak to me after that. Still, I figured I had made my point.

Another thing that baffles the international masses is your love of being war re-enactors, especially for the American Civil War. Goodness me, even I know who won that war.

Yet you still have a uniform-of-days-gone-by obsession, and it's not just me who thinks your costume fetish is weird. It's an international opinion. Take for example an incident that I was privy to in Scotland in the 1990s.

I was studying for my journalism degree and had the good fortune to do a semester at Napier University in Edinburgh. My video production class was headed-up by an American teacher who gave the class an assignment to produce a 30-minute TV travel-style program comprised of five minute segments highlighting things to do in Edinburgh.

The class then brainstormed ideas for individual segments. One clever fellow suggested a story on the one-o'clock gun that is fired at Edinburgh Castle each day. Another person suggested a story on the massive butterfly enclosure near the city.

Then one smart kid suggested a story on the Highland Re-enactors – you know, those folk who dress in a kilt, carry over-sized swords and run around the heather screaming 'FREEDOM and pretending they are Brave Heart?

Someone else said "What's their proper name?" and the class sat there collectively for a few minutes trying to think of the formal name for Highland re-enactors until some smart-arse yelled out "I know! They're called Americans!"

So there you are. The world sees you as a bunch of ye-oldie-dressing war-re-enacting-misfits who can't let go of the past and can't come to terms with their present identity.

On the up-side though, you do have a lot to be recognised for.

You were the land of hope for the oppressed, the poor and the down-trodden when the world had turned its back on them. You remain the defender of the oppressed as witnessed by the innumerable military interventions by the US to stop the spread of tyranny.

Within a few centuries you have gone from colonial outpost to a superpower and the defender of the free world. You make awesome sandwiches, you spread global joy with Reese's peanut butter cups and you can make a really fantastic car when you put your mind to it. What's more, you almost speak English. Who can't love that?

Therefore it is my humble opinion that it is good to be an American. So don't qualify yourself. Stand tall and proudly boast "I am an American".

If your announcement bores your listener then boo-hoo to them - they are probably Canadian anyway. If your listener is a radical terrorist lusting to kill an American then tell then you are an Australian with a bad head cold, hence your non-Aussie accent.

We won't mind.

Chapter 16: Staying in Australia

Hopefully by now I have convinced you that Australia is your ideal get-away destination. So pick up the telephone right now and call Qantas to book your flight - I know you want to.

Just make sure you have your un-refundable ticket first, then grab a coffee and sit down in a nice comfy chair before you read the next bit.

Ahem, I have something rather startling to tell you: Australia isn't America.

To prevent those eyebrow-raising moments following your arrival in Sydney I suggest very strongly that you read the following words of wisdom to prepare yourself for our way of life and culture.

Driving and cars: For goodness sake NEVER tell an Australian that we drive on the wrong side of the road. That's the fastest way to get a knuckle sandwich (i.e. a punch in the mouth). We just drive right-hand drive cars on the left-hand side of the road just like in Britain, Japan, South Africa and India.

This does cause some concerns for American drivers used to having the wheel on the left side of the car and it may even make you a bit scared of driving here in Australia.

I totally understand you because once I was made to drive a left-hand drive people-mover van by a bossy British Army officer in Germany as I was the only enlisted soldier in our group (British officers always give the crappy jobs to the peasant colonial soldiers). I had never driven a left-hand drive vehicle before or a car with the gearshift on my right.

I was justifiably terrified as I drove out of the airport, through a city and onto an Autobahn.

With a white-knuckle grip on the steering wheel I drove along with crazy Germans zipping past me. I just kept muttering to myself 'keep the passenger in the gutter' in order to keep on the correct side of the road.

That worked really well and I recommend it to you. The only catch is roundabouts – you tend to go around them the way you would at home. So just remember, if you screw up in a roundabout here in Australia then you are about to make your next of kin very wealthy if you have life insurance.

Toilets: I highlight this item because it's one you will use daily. I don't want to shock you but our toilets are different. We use half-flush and full-flush buttons instead of a lever. The pan is a different shape, the flushing water enters and exits the bowl slightly differently and the exiting water does spin the opposite way. I know it's crazy but our toilets still work and they save a lot of water. Please be kind and just use the damn thing without bursting into fits of laughter.

TV: The first thing that takes a lot of getting use to is that most Australians don't have pay/cable/satellite TV at home. We have a perfectly good free-to-air digital network with enough channels to bore anyone silly. I personally refuse to have cable TV in the house because given all the pay channels and content available I would sit there and watch something all the time. I don't want that because I want to get out of my house an experience something called 'Life' before it passes me by.

Because of our history we still enjoy lots of British comedies and dramas, plus we make a lot of TV shows ourselves. While there is still a lot of US TV on the tube you will probably find British and Australian comedy a bit hard to fathom. Try watching a few British/Australian movies before you depart to help with the cultural adjustment.

Religion: The national pastime in Australia is apathy so we don't go in for religion in a big way. We don't enjoy religious pontificating and we will use our God-given right to ignore you if you drone on about religious freedom of speech. We respect the right of the individual to pursue their own religious choices, just don't bring it up in government schools and in politics or you will see Aussies turn ugly very quickly.

Tipping: Guess what? We don't really tip in Australia. This is because we are more socialist than in the US and as such we have Government-mandated minimum wages that takes service into account. Some hospitality people would like you to tip because gratuity is always a bonus but it is unnecessary here. When asked for a tip I always say "be good to your mother."

Goods and services taxes: We have a 10% Goods and Services Tax (GST) here in Australia, but it is already built into the price you are asked to pay. So for everyday bills and purchases the price you see is the price you pay. The receipt might explain the GST component you just paid but the price on the box is the total price.

The GST component is always the same from state to state because in Australia the Federal Government collects the GST on behalf of the states and then redistributes it. This can be very difficult for Americans to get their heads around and I am not being cheeky. It is a very different and uncomplicated tax system that seems to have been sent to Earth by caring Martians. So while things may seem a bit more expensive in Australia at first, by the time you eliminate the U.S. system of added taxes and tipping you end up pleasantly surprised.

Police: Each state plus the Federal Government has a police force. That's it. There are no state troopers or sheriff's departments. The policeman in far-western New South Wales works for the same police department that operates 500 miles away in Sydney. Mind-boggling, isn't it?

Food: A lot of food that Americans take for granted are in limited supply or non-existent here. American-style cheese, bacon and Italian sausage meat are difficult to impossible to get. Forget about Root Beer (I'll tell you why soon) as well as Skippy and Jif peanut butter. Reese's peanut butter cups are around but hard to find, which is awkward for me as I am addicted to them.

While we do have McDonalds, Pizza Hut and KFC in Australia the menu and tastes are somewhat different. Taco Bell is basically nowhere to be found and Burger King is called Hungry Jacks. We do love Mexican food but it's not as common as in the US. Jell-O is called Jelly and your Jelly is called Jam. I know this all sounds like a great cuisine tragedy but it is part of the reason you travel overseas, i.e. to experience another culture's way of doing food.

On the plus side you do get to sample kangaroo, crocodile and emu meat. We have excellent beer and of course there are our world famous chocolate biscuits called Tim Tams, which are the closest thing to heaven you can eat.

Lounge Room: My American wife told me to put this one in. She finds it odd that we call the living room the lounge room. I think it makes sense because it's the room with the lounge chairs, which is what we call sofas. My wife thinks this is another absurd piece of English because a lounge chair is found in the yard or by the pool. Thanks to my apathy it really doesn't bother me. Anyway, she will clip me over the ear if I don't put lounge room on this list, so here you go.

Electricity: We use a 240-volt AC electrical system here and many of our electrical plugs are fitted with an earthing/grounding pin. If you plug your 110-volt DC American appliances straight into our sockets then it will go BOOM and die. Make sure you have a plug adapter with a voltage transformer or buy appliances here. Our electricity outlets also have a switch and our light switches work in the opposite direction to yours. Maybe it's all because being in the Southern Hemisphere we in Australia are upside-down on the planet compared to you guys.

Firearms: We love gum nuts and we hate gun nuts. The seed-nuts from our gum trees are cute, however guns are ugly and we don't have a constitutional right to bear arms (or to arm koala bears for that matter).

After a rather horrible gun massacre in Tasmania in 1996 we banned automatic weapons while handguns have been almost impossible to access lawfully for over a century. As a result we have little gun crime in Australia. What gun crime we have is dealt with by the police.

This is probably the hardest thing for Australians and Americans to understand about each other. We don't get your love affair with weapons and you can't see why we wouldn't keep a gun in the house. It's a very emotive issue so the best thing to do is accept it and not go looking for designer-colour pistols at Wal-Mart during your stay. It's easy to avoid because we don't sell pistols in department stores and Wal-Mart doesn't exist in Australia.

Abortion: Abortion is legal in Australia and tightly controlled. Australians on the whole do support a mother's choice; the argument is more over when during a pregnancy it should be allowed. It's another touchy subject to steer clear of.

American expressions: Some of your favourite expressions don't translate very well in Australia. A couple to keep in mind are 'root' and 'fanny'. In Australia 'root' means to have sexual intercourse and a 'fanny' is what a women has down below on her front-side (we also call it a 'Map of Tassie' [Tasmania] because with hair it looks like one).

So if you 'root for a team' we'll think you are a bit loose with your morals. If you fall flat on your fanny then we will look at you and wonder how that is possible, especially if you are a bloke.

Gambling, Alcohol and Drugs: Gambling and booze are everywhere and the national age for access to both is 18. Drugs are heavily frowned upon here and there is no medicinal marijuana - sorry dudes.

Silly place names: Many of our states and town names are from Britain and were applied by homesick convicts and free settlers. Some places are named for British Royalty (e.g. the states of Victoria and Queensland) and some places are named for leading politic figures and public servants (Melbourne, Brisbane, Ayers Rock).

Many have Aboriginal origins such as Parramatta and Woolloomooloo (which has been suggested as meaning 'a young kangaroo leaping through the air while being hunted'). The funniest names are double-names such as Wagga Wagga, Curry Curry and Woy Woy. In the case of Wagga Wagga the 'Wagga' means crow, so Wagga Wagga means 'the place of many crows'.

To be a true Australian you have to understand that it is perfectly OK to call Wagga Wagga 'Wagga' and to call Curry Curry 'Curry', but on no account ever should you call Woy Woy 'Woy'. This is perfectly true but I am totally unable to explain why – it's an Australian thing.

****

In summary, don't worry too much about Australia. We are a pretty harmless bunch but we are a bit eccentric, we do things a bit different and you won't always get the same products and services as you would in the US, but that's the beauty of travelling – you see and experience new things.

Just don't buy a didgeridoo when you are here. It's OK for Aborigines to play them because they make them sound cool. However, when a tourist plays one we tend to lose our temper because you make them sound like a platypus' mating call – it ain't exactly music.

Chapter 17: Dinner Party

I have this belief deep inside of me that is unshakable but not wildly known. I'll share it with you Yanks because you're a top bunch of folks.

When it comes to being a man I think there are two things that should be accomplished to prove your manhood if at all possible:

1. To have served your country in some way, such as in the military, police, fire service, emergency services or similar, be it full-time, part-time, volunteer or whatever. It only needs to be for a short period such as of a couple of years or so.

2. To have a trade of some description, e.g. a plumber, electrician, carpenter, mechanic, house painter and so on.

Now, this is not my mandatory legislation for all of mankind as it is difficult to achieve. Plus, not everyone has the health to undertake this self-development odyssey. I also think it is only a set of optional tasks for a woman as they already have the toughest job in humanity through bearing and raising children. It's just my thoughts and don't raise a head of steam if you think I am being an idiot.

Anyway, I have already overdone the first task by spending over 30 years in the Army. So that item is ticked off the list.

Now I come from a long line of blue-collar workers and a few years back I realised that my generation would be the first in my family tree to not have a tradesman among them. While I was grateful for the opportunity to serve in the military and to pursue a higher education I thought it was a bit sad that I didn't have a salt-of-the-earth civilian trade.

So three years ago I started studying commercial cooking part-time at the local technical college. I'm not so sure that I want to work as a professional Chef for a living because the work hours are lousy if you want to spend time with your family. However, I decided I could make my family and friends happy by producing restaurant-quality food and I could teach my children about healthy cooking.

I should have conducted a survey first because it turns out what everyone wants is a plumber. So I goofed there but I persisted with my studies and also worked in restaurant kitchens part-time to get hands-on experience.

I have now graduated with a Certificate III in Commercial Cooking, so I am a bit pleased with myself. I have also taken a fancy to, and have studied, French cooking because French technique is to cooking what American know-how is to nuclear submarine making. I am always on the lookout for an excuse to throw a dinner party and I thought I'd share with you a list of great Americans still among us who I would love to invite to dinner because I reckon that are champion ambassadors for the Land of the Free.

In no particular order they are:

Bruce Willis: Bruce has taught me a few things. First, you don't have to be handsome to be a star, just rugged. Bruce is a genuinely funny guy and I love his comedy work. I also deeply admire his dedication to the armed forces through his USO work. I am particularly proud of how he continues to work against ageism and produces great programs that show our later years can still be packed with fun and adventure. Finally, the humility he showed following his break-up with Demy Moore and his unflinching support for his children is beyond compare. I declare Bruce Willis an honorary Bloke.

Sandra Bullock: I had a poster of Sandra on the wall of my university accommodation in the mid-1990s and she hasn't grown a day older since. I like her for so many movies, especially her comedies, and I respect how she has taken the bull by the horns as a producer. She's beautiful, smart, talented and a role model to millions of girls including my own daughters. Please Sandra, come to dinner!

Kenny Chesney: Kenny Chesney is living proof that country music doesn't have to suck. I defy anyone to listen to listen to Ain't Back Yet and prevent their foot from tapping along. It can't be done nor should it be prevented in the first place. Kenny makes me feel like I am an American whenever I listen to him. I discovered his music on an Australian jukebox independent of my American wife and I admire Kenny's support for Farm Aid in the U.S.

Condoleezza Rice: This lady is without a doubt one of the most brilliant Americans ever. She was a superb diplomat and remains a gifted political scientist. I have heard her speak to assembled troops and dignitaries on an official visit to Australia and I was awed by her ability to speak very eloquently from the heart and without a single speech-note. She is also a brilliant pianist so I could save a few bucks and have her play show tunes while I serve coffee (I am very fancy-shmancy and I have a baby grand piano in my house).

Bill Gates: Bill has made such an impact on the life of millions of people and I particularly want to hear him talk about his philanthropic work and his views on what we can achieve to alleviate human suffering. Say what you like about the man but if we had more people like Bill in the world then the world would be in safe hands. I also reckon he would join in on the after-dinner song-fest because he still has a cheeky smile that means he's ready to let go when there are no cameras about.

Dolly Parton: The main reason I want to invite Dolly Parton is because she is a hilarious public speaker! Honestly, I am certain that if you spent one hour with her over lunch your face would ache so much from laughing that you would need to take two days off from work just to recover. She is also a leading example of defying ageism. Just imagine the after-dinner sing-along with Dolly singing 9 to 5 with Kenny Chesney singing harmonies and Condoleezza Rice playing honk-tonk piano. Absolutely priceless!

Michael J. Fox: Michael is a dual Canadian-US citizen and it is for his American accomplishments that I dearly want him to attend my dinner party. Michael and I are similar in age and as I grew up from teenager to adult I used first his acting career, followed by his books and his advocacy for Parkinson's disease research, as a yard-stick to measure my own life's accomplishments against. He has been a role model to me and his humanity, humility and optimism still serve as a guide to how I should behave. He is a devoted husband and father; my life would be a whole lot richer if I could spend a couple of hours with him.

Michelle Obama: Michelle really sets the standard for what a young 21st Century American First Lady should be like. She is a wonderful mother, a loyal wife and an amazing person in her own right. She is articulate, funny, ready to speak her mind and inspirational. I did think about inviting her husband but he is such a busy man and I think Michelle might secretly like to get out on the wallop (i.e. go drinking) and just hang with other Americans and a funny sounding Australian who won't report what happened on their Facebook page. Besides, I'd like to hear her sing a sultry ballad as she drapes across the piano and enchants the gathered guests.

****

So, what's on the menu for my esteemed American friends? I'm glad you asked, but just remember that in Australia an Entrée is a starter, not a main course:

Monsieur Jamieson's Fancy-Arsed French Dinner Menu for Legendary Americans

Entrée: French Onion Soup made without resorting to ready-made-soup-in-a-can

Main: Authentic French Cassoulet made fresh from the contents of the imported can I bought at the fancy deli (i.e. specialist delicatessen)

Dessert: Crème Broulee, where the sugar topping is caramelised with a military-grade flamethrower

Cheese: Whatever cheese selection box is on sale at the supermarket deli served with Made-in-France stale bread squares

After: Fresh Madeleines made with Vanilla Beans served with reasonable quality plunger coffee (I am good at making Madeleines just quietly)

Drinks: Your choice of 'Hop To It Lager', 'Chardonnay in a Box' or 'Cheap as Chips Merlot'

Bon Appetite…

Chapter 18: The Bit at the End

It's time to write the bit at the end of the book, so I'll crack on with it.

The thing I liked most about writing and researching this book has been the ability to focus on what it means to be Australian. I guess you tend to take your surroundings for granted after a while, so it has been refreshing to look again at my country and fellow citizens and then try to describe them in a way somewhat accessible to Americans.

We Aussies are a funny lot of bastards who occupy a unique place in the world, both geographically and philosophically. That said, we do have our serious side to our thoughts and attitudes so I hope I have encapsulated these for you too.

If there is one thing I hope you have learnt from these ramblings it is that there is a genuine affection in Australia for the US. Your music rocks hard, your cars roll fast and your Reese's peanut butter cups are proof of your culinary genius. You are the bearers of the torch of freedom and we think you Yanks are really top mates and we want to see more of you.

I hope you do decide to come and visit us because the welcome mat will always be there for you. I'm sure you'll laugh your arse off while you are here and then return to the good-old U.S. of A with enough stories to thrill generations of your descendants. Plus you would have developed a taste for Australian wine, beer and Tim Tams which your mouth will spend the rest of forever thanking you for.

Just to finish off I have one little story left for you. I didn't have anywhere else to put it and I think you might like it. This story helps describe the difference between the Australian Army and the Royal Australian Air Force.

When I was a lad I spent time in the Royal Australian Air Force's cadet corps, sort of like the Air Force's own version of the Boy Scouts for teenagers. I loved it; we did a lot of field training and we mucked about with aeroplanes to our heart's content.

Ever since primary school (elementary school) I had dreamed of being a fighter pilot, who we called knuckleheads. This was because in the days of early jet fighters only a knucklehead would strap a rocket to his arse and light the fuse. Anyway, this was not to be as I didn't finish high school as per social expectations. At the age of 17 I did join the Army Reserve as an infantryman, and later I moved into the Regular Army as an Air Dispatcher (sic), a soldier who prepares equipment for airdrop plus trains as a paratrooper so he can jump after the equipment and help get it ready for battle on the drop zone.

At least this allowed me to play with aeroplanes, even if they were propeller-powered cargo planes. On one occasion I went with an air dispatch team in an Air Force DHC-4 Caribou transport aircraft to New Zealand for an exercise. The Caribou was great for rough airstrip work but it almost flew backwards in a headwind. These aircraft had been used by the U.S. Army and U.S. Air Force in the Vietnam War and we had hung onto our Caribous because we like antiques in the Southern Hemisphere.

Anyhow, on our way home after the exercise and having spent seven hours crawling through the sky we were only half-way home, so we pulled into Norfolk Island to refuel. Having lounged in the plane's cargo bay for the trip I offered to climb onto the aircraft's high wings and refuel the plane for the tired aircrew.

A civilian contractor turned up with a mini-tanker and just as I was about to pump the gas I saw "Jet A-1" in large black letters on the tanker.

Being as sharp as a tack I said to myself: "Self, that's not right is it? That would be like putting diesel fuel into a petrol-fuelled car except we will be out at sea when the engines pack-up and we would crash into the sea, never to be seen again."

I looked to the rear of the aircraft and saw the aircraft's loadmaster leaning up against the fuselage looking like a later-day James Dean (I must admit, the Air Force chaps are a bit vain).

I called to him and said "Oi, this isn't right, is it?"

He took one look and screamed "For the love of God, NO!"

We sent the driver away as he muttered "I thought everything took Jet A-1" but he soon returned with the correct gas for piston-engine planes and I finished my task. The Air Force pilot and my Army sergeant were waiting for me, and this is where I learnt the difference between the two services.

Air Force Pilot: "Thank you for spotting that error Private Jamieson, you have avoided what could have been a serious accident. Well done."

Army Sergeant: "Well Jamo, at least you didn't screw-up today."

Come to think of it, I reckon the same sort of difference exists between the U.S. Air Force and the U.S. Army.

Hmmm. Perhaps Australians and Americans are two very similar sorts of people after all.

Glossary

Arse   The same as Ass, we Aussies just spell it better

Billabong   A rather fetid swampy body of water that was once part of a creek or river and is now isolated from the fresh-flow of water

Bonza   Fantastic

Bunyip   Mythical Australian devil-beast that inhabits watercourses. Of great cultural significance to Aborigines

Couldn't give a toss   Couldn't care less

Cow-Cockey   A Farmer – they spend their day talking to cows and cockatoos

Dodgey   Unreliable, untrustworthy

Down Under   Australia

Drongo   A rather stupid person

Drop Bear   Fictional carnivorous koala

(To be)Full-Bottle   To be fully informed on a subject or task

(The) GAFA	The Great Australian F*ck-All: the dead heart of Australia
(Have a) Gander	Take a look at
Get on the Wallop	To go drinking
(The) Good Oil	Some rather valuable information
Great Southern Land	Australia
Hoop Snake	Fictional Australian hunting snake
Land Down Under	Australia
Mum	Mom
Nifty	Clever, good
Yank	Any American, we don't distinguish between North and South as we heard the Civil War is over

Addition Australian expressions are explained in Chapter 9

Made in the USA
Monee, IL
26 November 2022

18668708R00059